The
Black
Aesthetic

Season III

TABLE OF CONTENTS

Re-t(reading) ground in Baltimore, an introduction
nan collymore

It means a lot to be involved in the editorial process of Season III of *The Black Aesthetic*, something that's come to mean so much to so many in the Bay Area and beyond. One of the most poignant experiences that we witnessed together was the "Affective Proximity" panel discussion between Arthur Jafa and Greg Tate at BAMPFA in 2019. I will forever cherish the question that TBA member, Ra Malika Imhotep, asked that sparked so much intensity and stillness in the auditorium that night. The ultimate answer from Jafa, or at least my interpretation, is that some of us, like he and Frodo are carriers of the ring. It's a good reminder that a keen focus on aesthetics and our relationship to production, and having them "seen," is incumbent often on the Frodos of this world. We have counted on TBA to wear the ring, while exploring their curatorial project of sublime and embodied narratives.

In thinking of Jafa, I think of TNEG, the film studio that he along with Malik Sayeed and Elissa Blount Moorhead,

Baltimore-based artist and curator, formed as a space for films and time-based installations to explore the interiorities and multiple subjectivities of Blackness. Blount Moorhead includes Baltimore as a character in her films and is interested in perhaps visualizing the "unseeable or veiled" aspects of quotidian Black life—something Jamal Batts, another TBA member, mentions in "Black Interiors: Intimacy." This makes me teleport to a city on the other side of the map to me and think of it in relation to my background in garment history, Black aesthetics and the interstices of the Black body and materiality. Hopefully I can weave a narrative that introduces this transmutative book, while telling a short story about Baltimore—a city I have yet to see, but love nonetheless because it symbolizes an unabashed Black interiority.

Michael Boyce Gillespie speaks of Baltimore in his essay, "Songs of Experience," on Ja'Tovia Gary's film, *An Ecstatic Experience* (2015), and her use of footage from the 2015 protests. In these few years since the beginnings (and end?) of The Black Aesthetic so much of the paradigm has shifted by way of Black interpolation of the camera in social media and its re-interpretation by artists like Jafa, Kahlil Joseph and Madeleine Hunt-Ehrlich. Black Aesthetics must be continually architecting and scaffolding a Black vernacular so we have ways to speak about this aesthetic that is a constant evolving phenomenon in Black life—hence my use of *Black gestural subjectivity* in the essay, "Grace Wales Bonner: Playing with the (non)body through dress."

In the city of Baltimore, visual artist Abigail DeVille walks the streets in her performed *Urban Migration* processionals, fabricated from the hands of whoever cares to join—an ensemble of beings in a blissful space of celebration. The same terrain that held the secret footsteps of families and more running and hiding along the railroad. The railroad is mentioned several times in this collection, first in Leigh Raiford's essay, "Death on Her Mind," where she mentions "Mr and Mrs Harriet Tubman," an unusually domestic depiction of a woman and her first husband, whose interior life we are often excluded from knowing, something artist Kerry James Marshall wanted to examine through color. Secondly, the railroad comes up in Arisa White's beautiful poetic offering ":: Broadcasting from the North Star, Harriet Isabella Truth, with Lady Luna & Nova Beatbox, presents *The Freedom Track* ::" as we maneuver across the landscape as fictitious "UnderGrounders." And it is this notion of the ground that I think of often as I address the streets of America, a land I was not born in, that leads me to think of how the city of Baltimore—a city of Black life, aesthetics and global capital—created a bestselling Nike shoe.

After only two years of exposure, in the mid-'80s Nike was withdrawing the Air Force 1. Baltimore, land that the Susquehannock lived on for several thousand years before the Europeans colonized it in the 1600s. Baltimore, one of few cities in America that is majority Black—African American, Cape-Verdean, Kenyan and Nigerian to name a few of the heritages that live there. Baltimore, not dissimilar to Brooklyn, Oakland or DC, cities plagued by the dislocation of sectors of the Black community, perversely described as "gentrification."

Dress is this unifier, a way of connecting to each other. In high school the wearer of black AF1's is seen as a person to avoid, untrustworthy, a potential school shooter, kids share this information amongst themselves as a way to protect and keep each other safe, the same way they did with the trench-coat, post-Columbine. But it's also a tongue-in-cheek/ ironic/Black-humor dig at style. In the same way dress identifies those not from a neighborhood, or newly arrived. In a city as complicated as Baltimore, the story of how it brought back the AF1 is only more compounded by Nike's recent uptick in sales. Contrast this with Baltimore's recent population and economic plight, intensified by the manipulative ping-pong played by right wingers use of disparaging and unqualified missives about infestation toward a Black population notably impacted by industrial blight, state-sanctioned violence and economic gains funneled towards a white minority—here the "See Black Women" manifesto exemplifies this in relation to an event in San Francisco.

Nike discontinued the shoe in 1984, but due to passionate local demand Baltimore shoe stockists fought Nike and encouraged them to bring the shoe back. And in 1988 the shoe returned to Baltimore, with lines forming from Baltimore residents and beyond, waiting for the rarefied sneaker. We don't know the names of the collectors, trend-setters and stylers who saw that the Airs was a forever shoe, those carriers of the ring—their names are lost to us. History serves the victor (the store owners) and not those faceless few who willfully wouldn't let them go. That's why we document—as Sasha Kelley has done by photographing TBA events, beautifully brought to life in this book.

"Nobody knows what Black people have contributed to the history of society."[1]

And yet everybody knows.

Black Lives. Black Aesthetics. Black Troubles. Black Stillness. Black Joy. Black Study. Black Silence. Black Movement. Black Matter. Black Sounds. Black Woes. Black Noise. Black-ography. Welcome to Black Interiors.

NOTES
1. Abigail DeVille, "Listens to History," *Art 21*, 2018

Black Interiors

In the Spring of 2020, The Black Aesthetic produced Season 4 in collaboration with the Berkeley Art Museum and Pacific Film Archive. With the support of BAMPFA film curator, Kathy Geritz, and the help of BAMPFA staff, we collectively researched, previewed, curated and screened films about intimate aspects of Black life that were found within the BAMPFA collection. To incorporate that experience into this publication, we have pulled together extended versions of the introductions given at the opening of each BAMPFA screening.

On Black Interiors
The Black Aesthetic Collective

We were overjoyed to be in collaboration with BAMPFA for the fourth season of our work curating film screenings that open up space for critical dialogue about Black representational strategies.

The films we showed were a little different from the material we had shown before. Season 1 took a DIY approach to showing films by and/or centering Black women, while Seasons 2 + 3 gave a platform to new works by independent Black filmmakers, many of them based in the Bay Area. Season 4 was presented in collaboration with BAMPFA's Out Of The Vault program. Through this collaboration, we were given license to treasure hunt through the Pacific Film Archive, culling through educational videos, news reels and other rare holdings in search of Black folks. And we were there. Known and unknown, narrative, documentary, and experimental, captured by cameras held in an array of different hands, across space and time.

Out of those findings we distilled a contemplation of Black interiors. What Elizabeth Alexander describes as expressions of Black life and creativity "behind the public face of stereotype and limited imagination."

Black interiors. The interstices. To be Black on both sides and on the inside parts. We invite you to glimpse this inside, this life world often denied. We invite you to read these texts resistantly. To understand the contexts of their creation, be it anthropological, educational, or artistic, as the field of play through which the Black folks on screen tell their own stories.

Spirit

Sermons and Sacred Pictures, Lynne Sachs (1989) ▪ *Georgia Sea Island Singers*, Bess Lomax Hawes (1963) ▪ *Yonder Come Day*, Milton Fruchtman (1976) ▪ *The Black Woman (excerpt)* [Black Journal No. 28], Stan Lathan (1970)

Spirit
Ra Malika Imhotep

> "You know, honey, us colored folks is branches without roots and that makes things come round in queer ways." —Zora Neale Hurston, *Their Eyes Were Watching God*

Spirit is Black radical energy. Spirit resides in and beyond the structure of the church. And, for Black folks, church is a room full of faith, of laughter and loud stomps, of community and Sunday Bests, of good gospel and good gossip.

In Lynne Sachs's, *Sermons and Sacred Pictures*, we are introduced to the work of Reverend L.O. Taylor, who captured the essence of the Black church in a series of recordings from the 1930s and '40s. In Bess Lomax Hawes's anthropological recording, *Georgia Sea Island Singers*, we meet Bessie Jones as part of a five person ring shout. Bessie appears again thirteen years later in the educational film, *Yonder Come Day*, as she corrals students at Yale and youth on St. Simons Island into a chorus of play guided by the games and songs of her ancestors.

Georgia Sea Island Singers, Bess Lomax Hawes (1963)

If we believe that Black spirit evades capture, how do we reconcile a series of films that purport to show Black culture and Black praise. A ring shout filmed inside the sterile Blackness of a sound stage is a queer thing. An early 20th century Black preacher's archive being entered and reinterpreted by a white woman filmmaker in the late '80s is a transgression of both time and the cultural sanctities of colorline. A Black professor at Yale urging his mostly white students to join in on the rhythms and play presented by a Gullah-Geechee elder is a bit awkward. Nikki Giovanni dares to tell a new creation myth, and all the while we are left to wonder what became of Bessie Jones, the Sea Island Singer turned cultural

The Black Woman [Black Journal No. 28], Stan Lathan (1970)

ambassador, her niece and the southern children she so desperately wanted to implore to cherish their own history.

Rev. Taylor's film footage and Lynn Sachs's contemporary arrangement of it give us a grammar for the appraisal of "sacred pictures." The term "sacred pictures" in and of itself sounds like the way somebody's Black grandma talks about both her precious family photos and the images of white Jesus looming over her living quarters. In this speculative anecdote, the sacred is both deeply familiar and holy in its foreignness.

In *The Black Woman* segment of the 1970s television program, "Black Journal"—from which we excerpted

Yonder Come Day, Milton Fruchtman (1976)

that Nikki Giovanni poem—there is a section devoted
to a Black church in Detroit called, "The Shrine of the
Black Madonna." Here, there is no white Jesus and the
most sacred picture is that of an ebony-Black woman
and her child. Following the political and cultural
mandates of the time, Black spirituality looks radically
different in the 1970s than it does through Rev.
Taylor's 1930s lens.

I recently discovered Black folk singer, Toshi
Reagan's, rendition of the Gullah-Geechee hymn,
"Yonder Come Day," and in the layering of her singular
Black queer voice I am taken back to the ring shout.
Leading me to make the essentialist claim that Black

folks are always about the business of making God(s) sound like themselves. While we first interpreted the name of the film, *Georgia Sea Island Singers*, as a generic description of the group, the Georgia Sea Island Singers were, in fact, a traveling folk music ensemble with a shifting roster of performers. Does the fact that this ensemble knew themselves to be performers, and were familiar with the anthropological gaze and capture of both ethnomusicologist, Alan Lomax, and his folklorist sister, Bess, make the picture less sacred? As we watched the beautifully lit troupe of Black elders in *Georgia Sea Island Singers* stomp and clap and sing and play—their skin silver against the manufactured Black of Bess Lomax's sound stage—they are clearly out of place. Yet witnessing them in the space of BAMPFA's Osher Theater, where my friends and collaborators were far out-numbered by strangers and white folks, I felt completely at home.

The Reverend Marvin K. White is a poet, artist, teacher, and preacher who offers in his writings, sermons and general presence a reflection of God's perfect love, and Black Jesus's perfect smile. He joined us on stage the night of "The Black Interiors: Spirit" program in a t-shirt featuring the cover art from the 1991 first-edition of *Brother to Brother: New Writing by Black Gay Men*, edited by Essex Hemphill. This sartorial choice, the Black Gay preacher dressed in the words of his deceased forbearers, is a ring

shout of its own. We could say that Marvin has a habit of coming 'round in explicitly queer ways.

It was the last week of Black History Month when we gathered to tend to each other in front of a large and mostly anonymous audience. There was laughter. There was "bibliomancy." A white woman was invited to face her feelings of alienation and, in a frenzy of emotion, proclaimed her love for Africa in a fit of tears, then stormed out.

And perhaps that is the function of "sacred pictures," all the feeling that exceeds the frame. The affect and haptics of witnessing a cultural act familiar in its pitch towards the unseen but deeply felt presence of something bigger than my own Black self. "Day done broke / inna my soul" the Sea Island Singers proclaim, bodies beating out every section of the rhythm. And it doesn't matter the context of the initial performance or context of my viewing, I am called again to reckon with an internal yearning to "steal away" onto my own horizon. ▪

PREVIOUS PAGE: *Georgia Sea Island Singers,* Bess Lomax Hawes (1963) ABOVE: *Sermons and Sacred Pictures*, Lynne Sachs (1989)

Intimacy

Pizza Pizza Daddy-O, Bess Lomax Hawes, Bob Eberlein (1969) ▪ *Relatives,* Julie Dash (1989) FEATURING: Ishmael Houston-Jones ▪ *This Is the Home of Mrs. Levant Graham,* Claudia Weill, Eliot Noyes, Jr. (1970) ▪ *Evan's Corner,* Stephen Bosustow (1969) ▪ *Slowly, This,* Arthur Jafa (1995) ▪ *Untitled,* John Sanborn (1989) FEATURING: Bill T. Jones

Intimacy
Jamal Batts

We can define intimacy, the night's theme, as a tight
and imperfect space, full of possibility. The films in this
screening linger on the line between the Black interior
as, on the one hand—the internal complexity of the
Black psyche—and, on the other, the arrangement of
the home, Black domestic space. Elizabeth Alexander
speaks to this intricate relation between Black internal
and external life when she writes that "the self is
made visible in the spaces we occupy," in "literal
'Black interiors,' the inside of homes that Black people
live in." Black people have long been profoundly
disconnected from ideals of domesticity, home life,
and its terms—mother, father, child.[1] It might be said
that the films we viewed are attempts at keeping the
Black head and home together.

That night we assembled in order to view the divinity
of the spaces Black people make with an eye toward
love. We have faith we are in the company of the all too
undercommon, who practice seeing and questioning
this complex world of moving images with a careful,
caring eye. We seek witnesses to the profundity of our
inside parts, our guts splayed, our Black Interiors.

TOP *Evan's Corner*, Stephen Bosustow (1969)
BOTTOM *Pizza Pizza Daddy-O,* Bess Lomax Hawes, Bob Eberlein (1969)

For the Black girls on an LA playground in the night's first film, *Pizza Pizza Daddy-O*, intimacy announces itself as a shifting formation of hand games and personalities. Intimacy here is to be a part of the circle. An all-knowing anthropologist's voice(over) declares that these Black girls' songs and gestures are derived from the British Isles. However true, these girls live in Watts (not that long after the riot) and their lyrics' discordant mentions of death and broken relationships, provide a kind of tenuous undertone to their often joyous chants. Their adaptive arrangements evince a movement toward happiness and hapticality that shirks the lifeworld, environs, and voices that attempt to determine them.[2]

Passing down knowledge through muscle memory is a theme that continues in director Julie Dash's experimental, *Relatives*, where dancer Ishmael Houston-Jones carries his mother's stories (and, indeed, his actual mother) on his back. After moving through a dream-like spatial and photographic rendering of his pastoral and grassy upbringing, Houston-Jones finds himself under the spotlight in an abandoned warehouse; maybe an off-key reference to his own personal (Black and queer) migration to the lights of the big city. However, his mother's voice is a lovely constant.

This Is the Home of Mrs. Levant Graham invites us into a nurturing and abundant encounter with the

PREVIOUS PAGE: *Pizza Pizza Daddy-O*, Bess Lomax Hawes, Bob Eberlein (1969) ABOVE: *This Is the Home of Mrs. Levant Graham*, Claudia Weill, Eliot Noyes, Jr. (1970)

Black domestic sphere. It is a film that makes me think about the invitation into a Black home; and the line between surveillance, documentary, and love. This is the moment wherein Black feminist critics were dissecting the ways in which the infamous Moynihan Report villainized Black women as the harbingers of Black familial dysfunction. The film starts with Mrs. Graham filling out an application in which she is made to describe the intricacy of her life by checking off boxes, indicating that she is separating from her husband and has multiple children. The adjective that

Slowly, This, Arthur Jafa (1995)

might best describe the shooting of the film is tight. Most shots are close, the camera is in direct proximity to the home's faces and object. This is a style chosen to mirror the condition of the packed house that looks to shelter many children and extended family. As Mrs. Graham so presciently puts it, "poor people can't live." They can't live the spacious lives of the white folks on the TV playing in the background of the Graham home; but they do live, and fight, and dream, and kiss, and love in all of the grand and sordid ways that people do (even when they are constantly being watched by white filmmakers). As with many of the films we screened in Black Interiors, the presence of white makers does not wholly determine the lives and creativity of those filmed. These evince the means

Untitled, John Sanborn (1989) featuring: Bill T. Jones

by which Black ways of being can sear away at the presence of a white gaze (if you let them).

A lushly filmed day in the life of a Black boy, *Evan's Corner*, asks how can we find and prioritize intimacy with ourselves, as Evan, our young protagonist, wrestles with his need for autonomy. Like *The Blue Dashiki*, an educational film screened during "Black Interiors: Sweat," the film follows an industrious Black boy working hard to secure something of his own—in this case, decorations for a corner of the apartment he shares with his parents and siblings. This corner is his mother's smart idea for giving Evan a sense of self in their quaint home. Evan wants "a chance to be lonely," waste time, and enjoy peace and quiet. He inevitably finds this occasionally stop-motion quest for propriety and individuality limiting and leans toward communal service.

In director Arthur Jafa's, *Slowly, This*, two friends reflect on the ways Blackness and gender impact their intimate lives. Two men sit at a dinner table at a trendy Manhattan eatery, at night, surrounded by the discontinuous elements of their mid-1990s cultural milieu. The patience with which these men—one Black, one Japanese-American—handle their difficult conversation is relayed in the film's pacing. Their navigation of how racialized gender impacts their most everyday and interior relations is harbored by the atmosphere's measured tempo. Smoke unfurls from a cigarette in a kind of organic slo-mo. The people of the time—a crowd sprinkled with luminaries including bell hooks, Isaac Julien, and Julie Dash—languish at the bar. At this table, these friends testify to the transformative power of honestly facing the place of masculinity in all of our lives.

And, in closing, we watched Bill T. Jones dance through the loss of his partner, Arnie Zane, in director John Sanborn's *Untitled*—an abstract view on intimacy with grief and the beyond. The eleven minute clip tears through the screen and grabs you by the chest. Bill T. Jones says, "Do you remember…" again and again to his late partner while looking through the camera. You are a witness to Jones's belief in the beyond he speaks to. It feels as if you are interpolated into this beyond. A testimony to the grief of the early AIDS crisis and the many souls whose presence it robbed us of, Jones here makes a special cinematic place for he and Zane's love; its presence in dreams and memories and, most importantly, movement. Throughout, Jones dances Zane's choreography, sometimes with a hologram of Zane. In the end, Jones states, looking at the camera, "I think we're alone now." The impact will take you outside of yourself. ▪

NOTES

1. See Hortense J. Spillers, "Mama's Baby, Papa's Maybe: An American Grammar Book," *Diacritics* 17, no. 2 (1987): 65-81.

2. Stefano Harney and Fred Moten describe hapticality as "the capacity to feel [through] others, for others to feel through you, for you," a form of "skin talk" or "hand laugh" in line with these girls' hand games. Harney and Moten, *The Undercommons: Fugitive Planning & Black Study* (Autonomedia, 2013): 98

Sweat

Apr 4, 2019

Right On/Be Free (excerpt) Sargon Tamimi (1971) ▪ *Finally Got the News*, Stewart Bird, Peter Gessner, Rene Lichtman (1970) ▪ *Noel's Lemonade Stand*, Carol Munday Lawrence, Mitchell Rose (1981) ▪ *The Blue Dashiki: Jeffrey and His City Neighbors*, Maclovia Rodriguez (1969) ▪ *Felicia*, Bob Dickson, Alan Gorg, Trevor Greenwood (1965) ▪ *Fashion photo shoot film roll*, Filmmaker unknown (late 1960s)

Sweat
Leila Weefur

Felicia, Bob Dickson, Alan Gorg, Trevor Greenwood (1965)

Sweat was the final screening of the Black Interiors
program, and the conclusion to the fourth season of
screenings organized by The Black Aesthetic. This was
the last page in a tri-fold of our curatorial imaginations.
This series was created as an invitation to the public
to witness the many interiors of Black lives and, to be
clear, not all which inhabit those interior spaces are
evidenced in the Pacific Film Archive.

TOP *Right On/Be Free*, Sargon Tamimi (1971); BOTTOM *Fashion photo shoot film roll*, Filmmaker unknown (late 1960s)

What we assembled was an abridged articulation of three of many Black interiors. Part one, *Black Interiors: Spirit* was the initiate, a prayer, a hymn, and a lullaby out of which an essence of Black spirituality materialized, a document of many visions, including Lynne Sachs and Bess Lomax Hawes. Part two was *Black interiors: Intimacy*, a space with many doors, some of which are readily open, some doors hidden in plain sight. The doors of intimacy were seen through the visionary minds of Julie Dash and Arthur Jafa, and explored through the imaginative journeys of children.

We sat together infinitely in the experience and discovery of *Sweat*. An interior space producing exterior effects. A space our body responds to with immediacy. Sometimes out of desperation, sometimes out of urgency for change and out of exasperation with the way things are. And so we sweat as an expression of what Kara Keeling refers to as "affective labor," which Maria Landy further describes as, "a form of labor expended in the consumption of cinematic images…A labor expended in order to produce and maintain forms of social life." Black social life.

Sweat is evidence of labor. The screening's films reflect the inner worlds of Black working people, asking us to consider not only the material outcomes of their efforts, but the moments of tension, pleasure, communion, and delight that give "Black labor power" its depths. We began with the political vibrancy of the

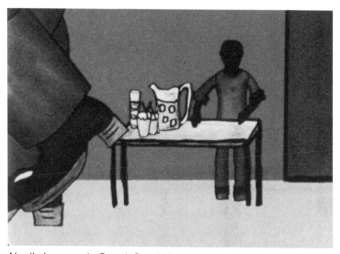

Noel's Lemonade Stand, Carol Munday Lawrence, Mitchell Rose (1981)

'70s. An excerpt from Sargon Tamimi's 1971 short film, *Right On/Be Free*, features the Alvin Ailey Dance Company's, Judith Jamison, dancing with the Brutalist architecture of the former Berkeley Art Museum & Pacific Film Archive building as a backdrop. The effortless and meteoric curves of her movement are placed in direct opposition to the severe concreted angles of the building, with The Voices of East Harlem giving us a choral Funk arrangement of the same title for sonic texture.

Connecting the counter-dialogues of 1970s radical Black movement with political movements, and the voices of urgency and protest, *Finally Got the*

PREVIOUS PAGE: *The Blue Dashiki: Jeffrey and His City Neighbors*, Maclovia Rodriguez (1969) ABOVE: *Finally Got the News*, Stewart Bird, Peter Gessner, Rene Lichtman (1970)

News, transitions to scenes of Black auto-workers in Detroit. Produced in association with the League of Revolutionary Black Workers, the documentary extends the architectural collision in scenes of Michigan's famous auto factories with the riotous ensemble of protest. Both films, effective in identifying how bodies can sweat in conviction, stand as a chilling reminder of Jack Halberstam's words in the introduction of *The Undercommons: Fugitive Planning & Black Study*: "The call is always a call to dis-order and this disorder or wildness shows up in many places: in jazz, in improvisation, in noise."

The Kathleen Collins-scripted animation, *Noel's Lemonade Stand*, the educational short, *The Blue Dashiki*, and the experimental documentary, *Felicia*, consider economic collectivity, self-sufficiency, and proto-Black feminist critique. The children depicted dream of possibility in earnest despite imminent dangers, and their labor is consistent in hubris and innocence. All three films locate the quiet cacophony to be found in children, though never dulling the sharp edge and palpability of their political objections. We ended with a short meditation on Black werk: a fashion photoshoot, because if history has proven anything, it is that Black folk know that work means *werk*, even if we sweat it out in the process. The camera is the machine to which we, in verb and gesture, express our *consent not to be a single being*, and proffer evidence of this boundless promise.

I find it most relevant that we gathered together in darkness to witness the permutations of Black intimacy, spirituality, and sweat, and, in the most intimate of spaces, the Black imagination. It was in a movie theatre where I discovered and cultivated my own interior language. I found the cinema to be a place, hidden in plain sight, where I could sit among other bodies, unannounced and in private. A place where, unlike home, I could take a pew, but unlike church, I could take a pew and find solitude without asking permission from God. It was in a theatre where I first realized the many ways Black people dream, the many ways we dream in lieu of sleep. Black interiors are a confection of dreams, be they dark or sweet, a delicacy made up of ways of being in our memories, within a parallelism of collective intimacy. Black interiority is found in an unbroken and consistent existence of gathering in cinematic darkness, it was found again with Jamal and Malika in our shared private desires to seek intimacy with everyone in the theatre. ▪

See Black Women

See Black Women was initiated as a collaborative response to the San Francisco Arts Commission's mismanagement of the Maya Angelou monument for the San Francisco Public Library in 2019. The decision to dismiss the selection panel's nomination of Lava Thomas's proposal re-inscribed the legacy of appropriation and misrepresentation of black women. The failure to acknowledge and address the Eurocentric conventions perpetrated by the legislative sponsors revealed the everyday normalization of the colonial gaze.

We are a movement of artists, activists, curators and writers raised on black feminist theory. We center the work of black women. We are a platform for self-representation free from stereotypical tropes of black women countering narratives that undermine the expression of our diversity.

S

e   e

b   l   a   c

k   w   o   m

e   n   s   e

e   b   l   a

c   k   w   o   m

x n s e e b l a c

k w o m e n s e e

b l a c k w o m x n s e e b l a c k

w o m e n s e e b l a c k w o m x n

2   0   2   0

raiford

thomas

ekundayo

hennessy

king

see black women

hear black women

trust black women

love black women

protect black women

pay black women

Statement Towards Conclusion I
Ra Malika Imhotep

The Black Aesthetic has evolved from a series of
DIY film screenings held in Oakland bookstores and
backyards and galleries to a curatorial collective that
stages provocative holdings of Black representation
across a broad array of locales. From two cousins to
four friends to six homies and now three collaborators,
TBA has moved through many different forms over
the past four years. In every configuration, Oakland-
based Black creatives have sought out to find and
cultivate a community engaged in the practice of
seeing Black people in all the different ways we show
up. I remember the moment I first heard about The
Black Aesthetic. Jamal and I were on the 6th floor of
Barrows Hall at UC Berkeley when he mentioned a
screening of Cauleen Smith's *Drylongso* (1998) at
Wolfman Books in downtown Oakland. Fueled by
excitement about the film that I had watched alone
in my basement studio apartment just a few weeks
earlier and a desire to instigate some Black queer
creative romance, I insisted we go. And what I found
there was much more than I had anticipated. There
was laughter, there was ego, there was anxiety, there
was curiosity, there was confusion, there was love…

Four seasons later, I'm trying to reflect on what this work has been and has meant and I keep turning on love. I can say, in integrity, that TBA was a labor of love and heartbreak. There has been all the thrill and excitement of being infatuated with a new thing, the deep yearning to be seen, the beauty and wonder and promise opened up by the breadth of conversations we were able to facilitate paired with the validation of being seen and appreciated by our peers and mentors. And then there were moments of frustration where it didn't quite click, where our egos betrayed one another and we scrambled to remember why any of it mattered. We've learned firsthand the ways working to make and maintain a Black arts collective can push you toward and pull you past your limits. And beyond your perceived limits, there is a whole world of new possibilities. Through TBA, I got to know myself as an artist and an arts writer. In response to TBA's call to curate public discourse through screenings and produce a new body of Black arts criticism in the companion publications, I freed myself to think, create and write in ways that were honest and deeply felt. TBA introduced and exposed me to a corner of creative community that I might not have allowed myself to explore otherwise. And here I have found something akin to home (with all its intimate joys and turbulence). As we compile what will be the final formal TBA publication, I move forward with so much gratitude for the lessons this work has taught and the opportunities it has created for everyone who has been a part of this collective effort.

I also feel some grief. I feel grief for the loss of this collective, this container. I feel grief for those who have watched and worked with us but are no longer here. I feel present to the way TBA brought a lot of us out of our silos into a space that felt alive. And I hope that moving forward we—everyone from collective to broader community—can hold on to that aliveness and our ability to create that, to *be* that, for one another.

Death on Her Mind
Leigh Raiford

One time I wrote a poem so fast and so good a man
who heard it told me it was like I had been ridden
by angels. Now I'm generally skeptical of religious
anything and I was certainly uncomfortable with this
stranger conveying to me his visions of my being
mounted. But I caught his meaning nevertheless &
couldn't exactly say he was wrong.

It was 1997 and I was living in a frenzy of creative
Eros, writing constantly, sleeping little, in perpetual
motion, so emotionally raw—by which I mean both
tender and unprocessed—that I was never sure if my
heart was breaking or bursting. Each person I met
was a muse and everything was all so hot and sharp
to the touch. I was living here and by here I mean
California which is where I call home now but then it
was there and so I was also living on borrowed time in
a future place, going full out every day until the day I
was supposed to return to what everyone told me was
my real life. It was clear that I was ready to produce
that poem which came so fast and so good and better

COLLAGE FROM "Woman With Death on Her Mind," Kerry James
Marshall (1990)

than anything else I'd written in my life up to that point that I became convinced that I just might die and it might be okay if I did. But I was 24 and to me death wasn't actually a thing, angels riding me or not.

Now I'm 44 and I don't have time for angels or poetry or muses or living so raw, by which I mean unprepared and naked. At middle age Death makes ever more frequent appearances. But I am skilled at keeping the tears out of my eyes & my skin cool to the touch. I've seen what happens when members of my bloodline give in to the angels who usually turn out to be devils. It ends poorly for them & even worse for the rest of us. When the frenzy knocks I've learned what to do: run or hike or sleep or go into the closet to cry. Bake or disappear into a museum. Phone a friend & drink, or drink & fuck my husband. And when that all fails, get on a plane.

Month before last, as sociopaths and Nazis prepared to take over the White House and the crack in the Antarctic ice shelf grew to 17 miles, I could feel the edges fraying. So I bought a ticket to New York and then bought a ticket to see Kerry James Marshall's *Mastry* at the old Whitney (now the Met Breuer). It is a show so brilliant, as in so glittering, that it takes three museums to show it and has basically forced a rethinking of the whole history of art. It is a retrospective so full of light that every time I thought I would be consumed by dark dark anger at how white supremacy has effectively consolidated its power through visuality especially through celebration of its own mediocrity, it was the sheer beauty of Marshall's work that opened all the doors and windows and let the light back in at every turn.

I could talk all day about "School of Beauty, School of Culture" or "SOB" or "Mr and Mrs Harriet Tubman" or "Black Painting" or the installation, "Art of Hanging Pictures," all of which read the Western art canon with such evisceration and serve us black life in loving large scale fabulist realness. "Mastery of form, deformation of mastery," as Houston Baker might say. Or, following VèVè Clark, "diaspora literacy" of the highest order. I was ready for all this, hungry even. But what was totally unexpected was a small early acrylic and collage on a book cover at the start of the show. When I saw "Woman With Death on Her Mind," I was shook.

Made in 1990, the piece comes early in the show, situated in the galleries of small works where studies appear, explorations of themes and methods that would appear in what would later become the signature works: the blackness of skin, the use of gold paint and glitter, symbology drawn from a range of histories and traditions. These rooms felt like prolegomena, the orchestra tuning up the opening phrases to a well-known and celebrated symphony.

"Woman With Death on Her Mind" is just that: a portrait of a woman's head with a skull resting in the architecture of her hair. Kerry James got jokes. I mean there is no metaphor here. Death is literally on this woman's mind, a second head that she carries with her. Yet "Woman With Death on Her Mind" manages to be both totally matter-of-fact and also full of conjuring. Death sits in the nest of the Woman's natural, giving the skull a home and a shrouded body. And in turn, Death gives the woman a third eye, divine sight. Indeed Death wears a halo golden and vibrant, whose light casts warm rays across the woman's face. It can't be an accident that both Death and the woman are black (a black skull when the Enlightenment tells us that all our stories rest on white bones?). Nor an accident that the woman's head is framed by upward green brushstrokes that end to reveal the tangle of vines and fleur-de-lis of the vintage book cover. And it certainly isn't an accident that both are smiling. Death & the Woman sharing a secret. You know about this, Leigh, they smile slowly at me… Wait was anyone else seeing this?

Kerry James Marshall had read my cards and then painted my fortune inside a book cover where he knew I would I find it. (It's hard for me not to read "Woman with Death on Her Mind" as Marshall's own space clearing for what would come next in his own practice.) Death rides heavy on my mind these days,

an almost debilitating fear of loss, loneliness, finality.
But here in Marshall's double portrait, I encountered
Death in the tradition of Vodou, as (black) ancestor, as
"fierce protector," as necessary to conditions of life-
making. Death and the Woman are symbiotic. A funny
kind of love story. In dark times now is the moment to
carry the spirits with purpose.

:: Broadcasting from the North Star, Harriet Isabella Truth, with Lady Luna & Nova Beatbox, presents *The Freedom Track* ::
Arisa White

HARRIET ISABELLA TRUTH
aka The HIT
aka High T
aka What Are You Waiting For?

Welcome to the month of bones,
when the stars and moon are fixed
in the heavens, I'm contemplating
freedom and design. UnderGrounders,
let me drop this shine:

Freedom is connection;
top-down-side its turning you,
down-up-side, you're dimensional.
You glow in a no-felt resistance to
how you stand, how you present—
you're solid truth, a body walking water.

You're in the justice of all things

without doctrine
without being pawned to a box,
    being cash crop,
    being object,
    being cha-ching.

Free from hollow,
from hashtag bars and branding—
our muscles with less and less memory
for sitting in the company of your face,
your frequency dully recalled.
We're tuned inhabitable,
visibly divisible.

UnderGrounders, roll-call your pieces
into your arms and sing,
Honey Child
Honey Child
You are beauty
You are seen
You are wanted
You can be
Honey Child
Honey Child

**::Lady Luna & Nova Beatbox harmonizes
darkness into diamonds::**

HARRIET ISABELLA TRUTH
aka Ain't I a Woman
aka Aint't You Human
aka Ain't Rockin Designs That Keep Us Profit

UnderGrounders,
Where you bound?

What you doing in the yarn?

Freedom is in the crystal clear,
the web undressed from its weaving—
transparent are designs
that cause us to approach
who we are in 4-40 hertz
in fear
doubt
red
orange alert

in the primal part of our minds.

Step barefoot on this:
We need our heart-chakra greens,
a pot-liquor love to release our wild,
vegetative life, our Fibonacci sequence seen
in all things—those natural forms
we give our attention to and become
compassionate I's.

The better to hold somebody's hand,
and their hand better holds a tree,
and that branch better holds the sky,
and the sky touches the ocean's skin,
and the ocean's skin gives a crab a lick,
and the crab better writes itself in sand.

::Lady Luna & Nova Beatbox births a loving ballad with its toes and hands, wings, and mountain streams::

HARRIET ISABELLA TRUTH
aka Your Mother
aka Your Mother Mother
aka Your Mother Mother Thrice

What say you, UnderGrounders,
if it's not Her name?

Free Her!
Every minute_____, every one in_____, every
    second_____, and right now_____
Her body is the first earth,
the prime conditions that act upon us.

Free Her!
that I n I

Free Our Femi Nine!
and therefore those
who've labored
before
and
before that
and that
and that
and ad infinitum equals—

          If she ain't free,
          there's no solving X, Y and Z.

**::Lady Luna & Nova Beatbox sotto voces vowels
of Freedam, Freedem, Freedim, Freedom,
Freedum, and sometimes Freedym::**

UnderGrounders, take your moment
of North-Star silence:

Freedom is surviving
sounds our tongues chorus—
notes from our a cappella bodies
constellate our outer spaces.
In the knowledge of D major,
free OM into the copious sky.
7-times-7 days and 7-times-7 nights.

Photography from Season III
Sasha Kelley

Numa Perrier at Spirithaus 10-5-18
FILMS *Jezebel* (Preview) + *Florida Water* and other shorts

Alima Lee at Betti Ono 10-19-18
FILMS *Brown* and other shorts

Benjamin Michel at Spirithaus 11-2-18
FILMS *I AM A GOD* and other shorts

ANKH ARTS PRESENTS

I AM A GOD

PROLOGUE

A FILM BY BENJAMIN MICHEL

Anisia Uzeyman at The Lab 10-26-18
FILM *DREAMSTATE*

Christian Johnson at BAMPFA 11-10-18
FILMS *A Moment of Truth + Sin* and *The Dutchman*,
Amiri Baraka, DIR Anthony Harvey (1966)

Creating Art in the Collective
Ricky Weaver in conversation with Michelle May-Curry

Over the course of the 2018-2019 season, seven Black artists and scholars gathered together under the mentorship of multimedia artist and MacArthur Genius, Carrie Mae Weems, through the Carr Center Independent Scholar Fellowship. Based in Detroit, the ISF program is designed to provide opportunities for early-career artists and writers to collaborate and receive mentorship from nationally and internationally renowned artists of color. Widely recognized as one of the greatest artists of the 20th century, Carrie Mae Weems was instrumental in creating a vital and dynamic experience for the collective, bringing not only her expertise but her generosity. As a result, what transpired throughout the inaugural year of the 12 month fellowship was more than anyone had anticipated; what initially began as a desire to create one exhibition evolved into a show in conjunction with the 2019 Havana Biennial titled, "The Spirit That Resides," and another in Detroit in conjunction with the opening of the Carr Center's new art gallery, The Contemporary, titled, "Beyond Space." Even after the close of the program, the collective (Nadia Alexis, Anita Bateman, Viktor L. Ewing, Michelle May-Curry, Ricky Weaver, and Andrew Wilson) continues to produce work together that pulls from the themes of the year's work.

Shod my feet in the preparation of the gospel of peace, Ricky Weaver, 2019.

Michelle: Creating work with a group of early career Black artists and scholars over the course of a year must have had a profound impact on you, as it did for me. How did the ISF collective inform your art practice?

Ricky: This newfound kinship has generated a whole new set of possibilities for me. Before this cohort I found myself growing weary. I seemed to constantly find myself in spaces where I had to educate and translate all of the content of my work. I had also been accused of hiding behind academic language in my writing. I was being required to explain while making sure to not over explain.

For the first time in a long while I was able to step outside of being "a black artist" and just make work with humans who had shared experiences. The relationships we have forged through this fellowship continue to flourish. We check up on each other while consistently advocating and making space for each other in our respective locations. It has been a blessing to grow alongside every single person represented in the group.

Michelle: Receiving mentorship from Carrie Mae Weems is such a monumental opportunity, especially for a Black female photographer interested in how the body appears in various spaces. What was it like to create alongside her?

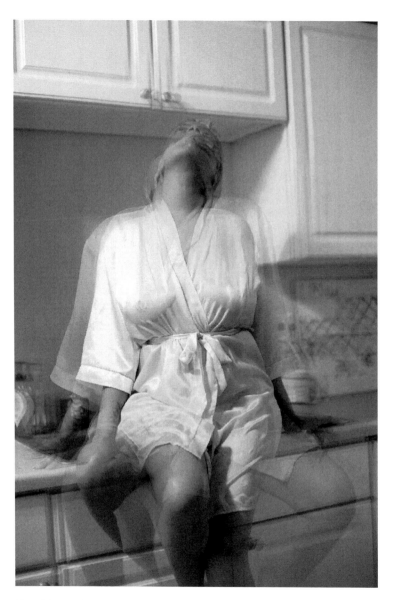

Breathing 1, Ricky Weaver, 2020.

<u>Ricky:</u> Carrie is the reason I shifted from figure drawing to photography as my primary medium. Her work has been integral to the very foundation of my creative practice. In the past I would refer to her as my art mother or auntie and look to her work for guidance. Working alongside her has been an absolute gift and I am still processing this dream. I have noticed a dramatic shift in my confidence as an educator and as an artist after watching Carrie transition through her many roles while maintaining a sense

of gravity. Much like within her work Carrie is very aware of her body and how she negotiates within the space she takes up. It makes sense that her images are able to hold the same weight without her physical presence.

INSTALLATION VIEW (LEFT TO RIGHT):
Shod my feet in the preparation of the gospel of peace,
Ricky Weaver, 2019.

Gird about my loins with the truth, Ricky Weaver, 2019.

Carrie has a very matter-of-fact way of simplifying concepts around making work and just being that allows one to "get out of the way of the work." In our first meeting Carrie spoke about a box as a metaphor for the concerns of our practice. She explained how we are always unpacking the same shit over and over. Very simple, but profound enough to affirm that I have always known what I was doing. I may not have always been able to articulate exactly what that box was as I am sure it will forever be evolving, but I knew and that's why it had to be made. The Kitchen Table series was the first contemporary art work that met me where I was. Carrie has done the same and I am forever grateful for her continued friendship and mentorship.

Michelle: The ISF collective produced two beautiful shows together in Havana, Cuba and Detroit, and a part of what made them so strong was how cohesive the themes of the exhibitions turned out to be. In Havana, the collective's work explored the relationship between spirituality and home, and was made even more impactful as the work activated an old home converted into a gallery space. In Detroit, the collective continued to think through home and space as both physical structure and spiritual presence. How do you see the themes of spirituality, home, and space continuing within your work?

Ricky: Spirituality will always be a site of inquiry for me as I am continuously unpacking and trying to recover the various ways in which Black women have found agency and mobility within their spiritual practices and in their homes, specifically the kitchen. It was the humming of a hymn that guided us across raging waters by moonlight. It was the undetected shards of glass that brought overseers to their end and made time for escape. We have reinvented technologies that allow us to remain unseen, like a spirit. In that context, there's something inherently spiritual about existing in the flesh of the Black feminine.

I source a lot of text from the King James Version of the Bible, Christian hymns, or familiar language shared by aunties, grandmas and cousins. I see no difference between the three as I see no difference between praying, braiding hair, or making a peach cobbler. This text is usually the undergirding context for an image that references sexuality, refusal, and something hidden. Ultimately I am interested in disrupting the archive to enable covert traveling through time and space for building and accessing worlds outside of now. I like to think of each piece as a negro spiritual[1], a signal pointing to a world that doesn't require escape. Freedom is a practice, we must always be on the move. I like to think of artists as conductors and ushers to the next where and when.

NOTES

1. Browne, Simone. *Dark Matters: On the Surveillance of Blackness.* Duke University Press, 2015.

Statement Towards Conclusion II
Jamal Batts

I must admit, thinking of The Black Aesthetic (TBA)
ending is difficult. It hurts, like the process of working
with friends, loved ones, and crushes is so necessary
and enjoyable but also hurts. I leave this long-short
and impactful experience with new loves and new
losses that I find it hard to balance. I remember my
first encounter with TBA, before I was a member. A
novel could be written about the multiple queer erotic
narratives that converged at that screening. It was
like my entire sex life, real and fantastic, met in that
room—a chronotope that focused as much attention
as it could on Cauleen Smith's *Drylongso* (1998).

I think a lot about the perhaps chosen loneliness
of being a teenage Black gay cinephile, traveling
alone to theaters in posh white neighborhoods to
sit in sparsely populated rooms to watch the latest
indie or foreign flick. TBA became a space where,
maybe, many traversed multiple forms of alienation,
mediated by screens, were able to create something
akin to community. Sitting in a small bookshop with
a group of opinionated and righteous fellow Black
creatives during our first season felt charged with
possibility. We had a diverse audience but those
who were nonBlack were most often lovely in their

ability to not take up space yet provide support. In meetings we would often joke about how post-film conversations were always filled with our voices. If a conversation got too hot, contentious, or specific to Black experience nonBlack folks would often get up and politely leave the room.

Like Smith's film about a Black woman traversing a state mandated deathscape through creativity, this experience also happened in Oakland. A rapidly changing and economically brutal city. The members of TBA were either raised in the city, born in the city, or transplants. We supported the work of many Oakland-raised artists but many of us, including myself, were also visitors to a city not our own, bolstered by various forms of precarious social and economic capital. I think some of the most difficult moments navigating my time in TBA derived from this nexus of members and our varying proximity to or desire for this capital or recognition. I think as Black creatives we deserve to have more conversations amongst each other (and with ourselves), to be clear about our varied intentions as we enter "the art world." TBA quickly became *a thing*, we were (in our various iterations) young, cute, and brilliant and came to know much of what was possible for us collectively and individually under that rubric in the 2010s.

I want to use this closing as a moment to encourage other creatives or folks with creative intentions (outside of the desire to create for pure self-fulfillment and the extension of established harms) to actually do it, with the knowledge in hand that you may have to let it go. Make the website, the Instagram, the newsletter. Have the long meetings. Be intentional and organize. Set your people free in all the directions that freedom calls for. Don't run from the consensual pain of it all but know your boundaries. Big love to Ra Malika Imhotep and Leila Weefur for continuing to make this work after all that we've been through.

Songs of Experience
Michael Boyce Gillespie

> "I am simultaneously creating and destroying, remaking and unmaking. My intimate interaction with the archive…expresses my desire to be a part of it, to make my presence felt in and on that history while also interrogating it." —Ja'Tovia Gary[1]

That which is beautiful and holy, an entanglement. Ja'Tovia Gary's, *An Ecstatic Experience* (2015), derives its title (and arguably its enraptured spur) from Kathleen Collins's, *Losing Ground* (1982).[2] Ecstatic experience is the research interest of Collins's philosophy professor protagonist, Sara Rogers (Seret Scott). Rogers works to conceive of ecstasy in ways more attendant to the artist's practice than to the strict terms of Christian doctrines. She must also manage the new ecstatic experiences developing in her life. As Rogers states while researching in the library, "If ecstasy is an immediate apprehension of the divine then the divine is energy." The energy of *An Ecstatic Experience* in total is a churning of performativities, affective economies, and temporalities. Black matter, a (w)holy syncretic revolution.

The film opens with found footage of Sunday morning people, black folk moving to and through glory. They come for His lesson. As the cross atop the church steeple makes plain: "He is alive again." With the readymade scenes of lost and found parishioners arriving suited and crowned, the rumors of an ethnographic ramble shifts to the metahistorical trace generated by the footage and Gary's manipulation of the stock.[3] The animation and score together refabulate and recompose these parishioners. This is call and response with an image and the capacity to sketch and conjure. Gary's hand processing of the film stock, her direct animation process, proffers a range of colors and shapes that regulate the worship beneath the frame.[4] Antibodies in motion. Escalation. Modulation. An anointing gesture, the animation on the film surface recodes the images of folks fanning in the heat, children sleeping, the preacher man preaching. "I'm just a vessel." Holy ordinance. They are folk fighting to keep the Devil from stealing their joy. Yet, as the film proceeds, it becomes clear that evil is not singularly incarnate.

Alice Coltrane's "Journey to Satchidananda" scores this section and compounds the vernacular faith of the previous section with transmogrification. The title cut from the 1971 album of the same name, the song begins with Cecil McBee's bass. A beat. A foundational pulse. A point of origin. And then Tulsi's tambura and Alice Coltrane's harp forge a harmonic counterpoint of strings that build texture and timbre along with the accents of Rashied Ali's drums. This orchestration builds to a synchrony of the concussive and the vibrational; a shaping stir of resonance and direction as the music settles into the stratospheric melodies of a raga swirl when Pharaoh Sanders arrives on soprano sax. A consecration is complete. Transcendental sounding. A sonic mapping of a new gospel boosted by the harmonics of conversion and ascension, a praise song in the black experimental idiom of jazz. Our text for today is the Word and jazz collectivity. Satchidananda. Ultimate. Satchidananda. Truth.[5]

Cutting from the rise of the spirit and rapture, the second section of *An Ecstatic Experience* begins with Ruby Dee on a television stage performing a slave. This is the "Slavery" episode for the *History of the Negro People* series broadcast on National Educational Television (NET) in 1965. Dee is a woman reminiscing about her mother's refusal to be a slave. She remembers her mother working in the field. She remembers her mother stopping and shouting, "Someday we ain't going to be slaves no more…I'm free, I'm free, I'm free." A black body at rest is a conspiratorial act. A woman caught the spirit and for that she caught cowhide lashes. Before suicide by cop, was there suicide by overseer? Ruby Dee

is reading an Ossie Davis penned adaptation of an
account given by Fannie Moore, a woman born a
slave in South Carolina in 1849. Ms. Moore gave this
account in 1937 at the age of 88 as part of the WPA's
Federal Writers' Slave Narrative Project.[6] During Dee's
monologue, Gary's animating hand on the surface
again engineers the diegesis beneath. The love below.
Remediation. Again, the animation stipulates process
and energy. Trembling. Cellular. Mitochondrial.
Animated shape fury. The shape of things to come.
Ruby Dee meets mitosis. Her image divides. Framed
by cubes and triangles. She is crowned, scarred,
erased. She persists. Speckled and haloed. Unbowed
and sainted. Transmogrification. Radiation ruling
the nation. Black matter. Two trains running. Two
freedom circuits. Two temporality scripts. A fusing of
a rebel slave and a Civil Rights celebrity, a memory of
resistance and a performative historiography.

From the Fannie Moore/Ruby Dee's remembrance and
hope for divine intervention, *An Ecstatic Experience*
cuts to a video of Assata Shakur speaking in Cuba.
A 1987 interview with Gil Noble for his long-running
"African American affairs" program, *Like It Is* (1968-
2011), Shakur comments, "I decided it was time to
escape…and that's what I did. It was a clean escape.
No one was hurt. I planned it as well as I could plan
it and that's all I have to say about it."[7] At the mention
of "escape," there is brief insert of Fannie Moore/

Ruby Dee from the previous sequence. In this moment flashes a historical continuum of shared resistance. An activist and revolutionary, Assata Shakur was a member of the Black Liberation Movement and associate of the Black Panther Party. Convicted of the murder of a New Jersey state trooper (1973) during a (disputed) confrontation on the New Jersey Turnpike in 1977, Shakur escaped prison in 1979. Since 1984, she has resided in Cuba since being granted political asylum: "Freedom. I couldn't believe that it had really happened, that the nightmare was over, that finally the dream had come true. I was elated. Ecstatic."[8] The terms of worship that the film first mounted with found footage refabulation and a testimonial memory of slavery now advances direct action and resistance. There are all kinds of prayer in this world.

From the deliver us from evil revival at the film's start to the Fannie Moore/Ruby Dee lenticular testimony of refusal to the free exile option of Shakur, *An Ecstatic Experience* closes on footage of Baltimore in a state of insurrection following the murder of Freddie Gray. Black lives matter. You think? This protest riot revolution disputes the quotidian shenanigans of black death. Gary's hand continues the treatment of the celluloid as fabric, a material dyed and cast. Her animation continues to stir as an instrument for improvisational and tinting historiographics. Chromopoetics. Haptic texturing. Scalar intimacies.

In this the film's final act, a chorale performance by Voices Inc., the group that stood on a riser behind Ruby Dee during the "Slavery" broadcast and performed throughout the show, is intercut with the Baltimore footage. The sequence's rapid intercutting produces a flicker effect as the group begins to sing "The Battle Hymn of the Republic," a song that timelessly calls out for judgment against wickedness. The quickened intermittence of the flashing facilitates the song's even bleed across spatiotemporalities and calls for justice between 1849 and 2015. Neural inscription. Affective acceleration. Escape velocity. "Glory, glory, hallelujah / His truth is marching on." Arcane and prodigious, *An Ecstatic Experience* deregulates the American archive. The film's historiographic circuit deliberates on worship, states of freedom, and resistance. Dead reckoning? Liberation cartography?

What do you call a film compelled by many stains/genealogies/materials/conceits?

~~Worldmaking.~~

Blackmaking.

Film blackness.[9]

Be anointed

Be still

Escape

Exile

Resist

Live

Fuck it, get free

A

black woman's hand…

NOTES

1. Ja'Tovia Gary, Personal communication to the author, March 2, 2017.

2. Gary is a member of the New Negress Film Society with Noutama Frances Bodomo, Dyani Douze, Chanelle Aponte Pearson, Stefani Saintonge, and Yvonne Michelle Shirley: https://newnegressfilmsociety.com. A collective of five black women filmmakers, they "focus primarily on works that break boundaries in film politically and artistically. Womanist in their content and experimental in form, often these are some of the most challenging for a marginalized filmmaker to create and distribute." Gary's nod to Kathleen Collins speaks to the re-emergence of Collins's *Losing Ground* through festival programs and revival screenings, a DVD release (2016) of the film that includes some of Collins's other work, and the discovery and release of her short fiction (*Whatever Happened to Interracial Love?* [2016] and *Notes from a Black Woman's Diary: Selected Works of Kathleen Collins* [2019]). All of this has produced a crucial and generative reappraisal of the history of black women filmmaking.

3. As Michael Zryd observes, "Found footage filmmaking is a metahistorical form commenting on the cultural discourses and narrative patterns behind history. Whether picking through the detritus of the mass mediascape or refinding (through image processing and optical printing) the new in the familiar, the found footage artist critically investigates the history behind the image, discursively embedded within its history of production, circulation, and consumption." Michael Zryd, "Found Footage Film as Discursive Metahistory: Craig Baldwin's *Tribulation 99*," The *Moving Image* 3, no. 2 (Fall 2003): 41. For more on found footage and ethnographic film, see Catherine Russell, *Experimental Ethnography: The Work of Film in the Age of Video* (Durham: Duke University Press, 1999), 239-272.

4. See Tess Takahashi, "'Meticulously, Recklessly Worked-Upon': Materiality in Contemporary Experimental Animation," *The Sharpest Point: Animation at the End of Cinema*. Edited by Chris Gehman & Steve Reinke (Toronto: YYZ Press, 2006): 166–178.

5. Alice Coltrane, "Journey in Satchidananda." *Journey in Satchidananda*. Impulse Records, 1970. See Tammy Kernodle, "Freedom Is a Constant Struggle: Alice Coltrane and the Redefining of the Jazz Avant-Garde" in *John Coltrane and Black America's Quest for Freedom: Spirituality and the Music*, ed. Leonard Brown (NY: Oxford University Press, 2010): 73-98; Franya J. Berkaman, *Monumental Eternal: The Music of Alice Coltrane* (Middleton, CT: Wesleyan University Press, 2010); and Cauleen Smith's *Pilgrim* (2017). Also, for a basic primer see Andy Beta, "Transfiguration and Transcendence: The Music of Alice Coltrane," *Pitchfork* (12 January 2017): https://pitchfork.com/features/from-the-pitchfork-review/10009-transfiguration-and-transcendence-the-music-of-alice-coltrane/.

6. Fannie Moore's account was published in *Federal Writers' Project: Slave Narrative Project, Vol. 11, North Carolina, Part 2, Jackson-Yellerday* (1936), 127-142, (https://www.loc.gov/item/mesn112/).

7. For more on black public affairs television, see Devorah Heitner, *Black Power TV* (Durham: Duke University Press, 2013).

8. Assata Shakur, *Assata: An Autobiography* (Chicago: Lawrence Hill Books, 1987), 266.

9. See Michael Boyce Gillespie, *Film Blackness: American Cinema and the Idea of Black Film* (Durham: Duke University Press, 2016).

Grace Wales Bonner: Playing with the (non)body through dress
nan collymore

> "The way he (Wilderson) recognises that what it is
> to be a subject is precisely to have a place in time.
> The term we use to describe that place in time is…
> the term we actually use for those coordinates is
> body. And that links it back to Spillers's work where
> the theft of body is the theft of a place and time."[1]

Grace Wales Bonner's bodies are stolen, they are
both inside and outside agency. To have a place in
time is to have a body, to be a subject[2], and Black
bodies do not exist, they do not live in the mythical
white supremacist/patriarchal version of history nor of
the now. This bodiless landscape is one that Wales
Bonner is meeting with—what I'm suggesting is a
form of Black gestural subjectivity—the language of
a garment's drape and flourish, this intricate dialog
between warp and weft has us decoding messages
through millenia, troubling the narrative of the
oNe. Her practice is one of merging differentiated
landscapes of time, culture and place, and this
"multiplicity of voices" is pivotal to her fashion text.

To categorize her as a designer of menswear is to limit her. She is erudite, a creator of a broad range of cultural product—she thinks, writes, makes, designs and meticulously mines each subject—building coherence in disparate phraseology. She does for the masculine what McQueen did for the feminine, boundaries levelled and skipped over by men in bare chests, shiny constellated jewelry and face-shielding chapeaux. Though, building her masculine imaginary landscapes from literary form has made Wales Bonner an incomparable architect in the world of fashion.

> "I never want to show a singular vision or a fixed notion. It's always about something that's more fluid and more shifting. And that comes through collaboration and interaction with other artists."[3]

Liz Johnson Artur
Édouard Glissant
David Hammons
Ishmael Reed
Jordan Hemingway
Aimé Césaire

> "This idea of brotherhood and interweaving all these different intellectuals and visual artists."[4]

Each season she paces from text to text to build her own dialectical framework. In the language she is speaking through her garments—there are curves and dashes and stutters that sparkle. Her work is a script that ripples down the wearers back, her garments are literary. We read her ideas through the swagger of dancer or model, through the collage she creates of the divergent influences that keep her in a prolonged state of dislocation. The bodies mirror the garments that adorn them, they are reflections of the men and the men deflect the image…it is cause and effect/call and response.

> "Dance is the universal art, the common joy of expression. Those who cannot dance are imprisoned in their own ego and cannot live well with other people and the world. They have lost the tune of life. They only live in cold thinking. Their feelings are deeply repressed while they attach themselves forlornly to the earth."[5]

Leroy, Joseph and Alanzo pour their identity into the steps that create "Practice," her Black gestural subjectivity in televisual form that moves across waters to hold her work and carry her shapes.

> "I feel like when I dance it's the true me that shines through, it's the most freeing feeling ever I become myself through the movement…inaudible …"[6]

She is making work that speaks to temporality and deterritorialization…the making of a Black queer topography that span generation, modality and place. She riffs on a Black mannishness, unpicking the cellular structures that make man a man. Her Black model wafts, shapes a narrative, a lexicon in his ineluctable Blackness-saturated catwalk and makes Black man the norm. How do we frame her silhouettes—butch, femme, cis, non-cis, cissy, homo? She is re-configuring men's silhouette—the flared pant leg, the Swarovski-bedecked headpiece, the models' bodies lithe and liquid in her intimate fabric choices and cuts. This "emotional dressing," this "soulful dressing" of being in between spaces, being one and none at the same time. She mimics movement of '90s dancehall and rare groove, speaking through the ages in a tongue she wasn't born speaking. Mast(e)ry.

> When you look in the mirror
> Do you see yourself
> Do you see yourself
> On the tv screen
> Do you see yourself
> In the magazine[7]

Her Black gestural subjectivity reflects the punk era, when what the protagonists wore was the language of anti-government, rebellion, personal addiction and internalized anger. Westwood carved those outlines referencing past heroes, while making poetic incisions and constructed verbage, "God Save The Queen"[8] and "Oh bondage, up yours!"[9] points to saving a particular aspect of British culture, as does Wales Bonner's discreet and gentle insertions of

116

cross-Atlantic contemporary British symbols—West African cowry shells, Indian paste gemstones and inter-cultural fibers. The political climate is similar, but she has altered the ways those activist identities perform, sewing the type into her garments, folding the message into the seam.

> "Heteronormativity functions as a form of public comfort by allowing bodies to extend into spaces that have already taken their shape. Those spaces are lived as comfortable, as they allow bodies to fit in; the surfaces of social space are already impressed upon by the shape of such bodies... Spaces extend bodies and bodies extend spaces; the impressions acquired by surfaces function as traces of such extensions."[10]

Dressing a particular body, giving that body opportunities to bend space and wander. Centering the Black male body into a femme discourse, moving parameters and giving space to an unpopular rendition, a widely-circulated/fabricated portrayal of the Black male. Troubling what Sara Ahmed defines as "being a question"—this perpetual state of conforming one's identity, of making one's self understood, breathlessly reconstituting self, in the eyes of the questioner, to the outside—giving space for gentle movement, taking time, languishing in materiality and making new shapes in the corporeal landscape.

Disrupting locations typically reserved for Black men performing a non-archetypal form of Black masculinity. Seeking an interiority and exteriority found in *Giovanni's Room*, this search for an internal/external home that James speaking through white David seeks:

> "There is something fantastic in the spectacle I now present to myself of having run so far, so hard, across the ocean even, only to find myself brought up short once more before the bulldog in my own backyard—the yard, in the meantime, having grown smaller and the bulldog bigger."[11]

Wafting over London, South Africa, Senegal, Jamaica merging the outlines of the cultural majority with historical English references—we are reminded that the colonized and post-colonized body is comfortable both in and out of dress, in and out of place. King stares back at us in hats with cross-continental influences, embodying Malik that "rebel of black fortune." His casual look reflects on Jimmy, neck scarf and taut, fitted, homilic denim.[12]

> "This idea of connecting with spiritual practices and rituals that originate in Africa and the Caribbean and observing how those threads are captured across the Atlantic."[13]

This Black visual mien Wales Bonner creates through the production of a linguistic framework of this Black body, this Black subject is an effect of the language she constructs of and with the body's text, making identity from the language of cloth, "the corporeal stylization of gender, the fantasied [sic] and fantastic figuration of the body."[14] The Black body, both in enclosure and out, will not be constituted, cannot be constituted because it does not exist, for it is stolen.[15]

"I just could always hear somebody running."[16]

NOTES

1. Fred Moten with Saidiya Hartman, J. Kameron Carter and Sarah Jane Cervenak. "The Black Outdoors." Discussion, Duke University, September 23, 2016.
2. Ibid.
3. Grace Wales Bonner. *Grace Wales Bonner: A Time for New Dreams*. 19 Jan 2019-17 Mar 2019. Serpentine Gallery, London.
4. Ibid.
5. Ishmael Reed, *Mumbo Jumbo*, (Doubleday 1972).
6. Grace Wales Bonner and Harley Weir, *Practice: A film by Grace Wales Bonner and Harley Weir*, 2017.
7. X-Ray Spex, "Identity." *Germfree Adolescents*. EMI International, 1978.
8. Vivienne Westwood, "God Save the Queen" t-shirt, 1977.
9. X-Ray Spex, "Oh Bondage Up Yours." *Oh Bondage Up Yours*, Virgin, 1977.
10. Sara Ahmed, *Living A Feminist Life* (Duke University Press 2017).
11. James Baldwin, *Giovanni's Room* (Dial Press 1956).
12. Grace Wales Bonner, *Portrait of a Muse*, Film commissioned by SSENSE, 2017.
13. See note 3.
14. Judith Butler, *Gender Trouble* (Routledge 1990).
15. See Hortense J. Spillers.
16. See note 1.

Parlor Room Sessions
Renee Royale

Creating as a Black person existing
on the Western Hemisphere
in 2020

          is to create from absolute imagination.

    As a descendant of survivors that were
not

        "intended"
        to survive,

it is my duty and destiny to create from my wildest
        imaginings,

    giving form to other creations that have never
    before existed; and would not, had it not been
    for

my existence + the existence of those who
        came before me.

        Survival, sustaining, is
        ingrained in both my artistic
        and creative practice as well
        as my DNA.

We are here to make
the

impossible possible, intangible tangible,

creating
everything
from
nothing.

And so it is.

.

Opening reception for Parlor Room Sessions,
Bushwick, Brooklyn, New York, April 7 2018. Photo
taken by Felícita Maynard on a Polaroid SX-70. Parlor
Room Sessions is an experiential art space that
mainly exists in Renee Royale's living room, and online
gallery. This opening took place on Renee's birthday
and offers a glimpse at the energy that saved her life.

Statement Towards Conclusion III
Leila Weefur

I was once ashamed to hear my last name
mispronounced in a room full of people. I was afraid
that I'd have to explain that I was Liberian, and cringe
when I had to correct people who thought they heard
me say *librarian*. I was afraid that being West African,
although born and raised in Oakland, would somehow
make me less Black than my friends but in that fear, I
found sanctuary in the imagination of filmmakers like
Ousmane Sembene.

Years before I settled into comfort with my body
and my queerness, I caught the censored version of
Cheryl Dunye's, *A Stranger Inside,* on BET. Though
somehow, still not censored enough to keep my
curious, adolescent eyes from seeing a woman's head
between another woman's legs for the first time. If
only I had known then that Dunye, too, was queer and
half Liberian like me I would have perhaps felt less
deformed and invisible sooner.

That moment when you think a single grain on
celluloid is small and insignificant and then you realize
that a single grain is a part of the cluster needed
to make a fragment of an image and it takes many
fragments of many images to make a film. That *bigger*

picture moment is the feeling I chase when sitting in a theatre or bookstore watching a film with people who feel or have felt just as weird and out-of-place as an isolated film grain. There is a home, afterall, for the cine-fetishists, Black or Queer or othewise reject-identified selves, alone together in the darkness. Floating like particulate matter in the stream of light being launched from the projector.

In many ways, The Black Aesthetic was a dream come true. With the same spirit that propelled the 12-year-old me to torrent films by Kasi Lemmons and Marlon Riggs, I helped organize a small community of people who could explore the depths of collective Black trauma in the name of cinema.

It was in the modest, Black-organized, Oakland spaces like Spirithaus Gallery and Nook Gallery where we squirmed in our chairs, dampening the seats with sensations of queer imagination and reveled at renditions of Black deity. I would later discover the genius of Dunye's *Watermelon Woman* and attempt to screen it during season one, only to feel the sting of our first rejection letter.

Our first two seasons, we had a projector on loan from E.M. Wolfman Books and a screen that could barely stand on its own tripod legs but we watched, we talked, and we argued until it was time to go home, for eight Thursday nights in a row. That first season, I was not an official member. I would just hang around and help Ryanaustin and Christian populate the list of films to screen, afraid that my Black wasn't loud and proud enough to host a crowd. Eventually, my longing to live in the dream overpowered my fear and I became part of a trio. The trio that grew to four, incorporating Zoé Samudzi, and then six, Jamal and Malika, to our final arrangement as a trio again.

What I find most remarkable about a collective experience, is how gestalt it is by nature. The participants, in this case, members—Jamal, Malika, and myself—each offers a perception of wholeness. The collective memory is a living assembly. In many ways, for me, this effort to forcibly make separate imaginations into a creative whole was a psychological reckoning determined to shape my understanding of the conditions of Blackness.

All of us have worked collectively and independently, to translate what we knew to be the manifold nuances of the Black experience. As a result of that process and the laws of proximity, we discovered parts of ourselves that lay within and outside of all of those defined layers. It's almost as if, with each season of screenings, the line connecting all of our creative disparities slowly grew definition until it wrapped itself around all of us and formed a distinct and rigid shape. The resulting shape, likely, appears different for all of us. But somehow, that shape holds together several lifetimes of creative vision, protects the short legacy of our dialogic exchange, and pronounces the possibilities harvested through Black collective thought.

It is funny that my interest has been to locate the boundaries and distinctions of Black existence while the collective goal has been to make known the expansiveness of it. I always wondered if dissonance was a necessary and unavoidable component of collectivity.

I think about transformation and how matter can affect and permanently alter other surrounding matter as a result of proximity. It is said that the gestalt qualities of something can survive even after the actual experience has faded from memory. Without hesitation, after a reflection of trauma, I can remember the distinct sounds of laughter that each member, past and current, let leave their bodies. After having fully embodied the experience of it, I understand how symbiotic and physically involved collaboration can be. Just as crying and laughing are a physiological process. Our celebrations activated the sinews of our bodies and reverberated just as vigorously as our failures, and accumulated in a sort of beautiful creative waste. But just as rainbows are never empty, The Black Aesthetic is never ending. That defined line has unwrapped itself and became a thread connecting everything we've done, and everyone we've done it with, to an infinite moment. The Black Aesthetic is forever in a state of TBA, to be announced, to be assessed, to be actualized.

CONTRIBUTORS

Jamal Batts is a writer, curator, and doctoral candidate in the Department African American and African Diaspora Studies at UC Berkeley. His work explores blackness, queerness, contemporary art, and the intricacies of sexual risk and risk-taking. His writing has appeared in the catalogue for The New Museum's exhibit *Trigger: Gender as a Tool and a Weapon*, *Open Space*, *ASAP/J*, *New Life Quarterly*, and SFMOMA's website in conjunction with their Modern Cinema series. He is a 2020 Robert Rauschenberg Foundation Scholar-in-Residence, the recipient of an LGBTQ Research Fellowship from the ONE National Lesbian & Gay Archives, and a member of the curatorial collective The Black Aesthetic.

Think of nan collymore's work as a gilded cloak that you wear, sometimes you're reading an essay, or hanging a garment, sometimes you're listening to a conversation. Her work is about the labor of love and the touch and the meaning that we move through when we are posing a question or troubling an idea…she uses her hands to compose thoughts through words/pictures and objects. She believes in magic and the sacred and conjures from the heart. She is often working with re-making and re-forming materiality into visual projects or palimpsests to re-frame a conversation on the interwovenness of subjectivity.

Michael Boyce Gillespie is Associate Professor of Film at The City College of New York, CUNY. His research and writing focuses on black visual and expressive culture, film theory, visual historiography, popular music, and contemporary art. He is the author of *Film Blackness: American Cinema and the Idea of Black Film* (Duke University Press, 2016) and co-editor of *Black One Shot*, an art criticism series on ASAP/J. His recent work has appeared in *Black Light: A Retrospective of International Black Cinema*, *Flash Art*, *Unwatchable*, *Film Quarterly*, and *Keywords in African American Studies.*

Ra Malika Imhotep is a Black feminist writer + performance artist from Atlanta, Georgia, currently pursuing a doctoral degree in African Diaspora Studies at the University of California, Berkeley. Her creative and intellectual work tends to the relationships between black femininity, vernacular aesthetics and the performance of labor in the Dirty South. She is co-convener of The Church of Black Feminist Thought, an embodied spiritual-political education project, and a member of the curatorial collective The Black Aesthetic. She was an Omi Arts Creative Arts Practice Artist-in-Residence at Ashara Ekundayo Gallery and a DAMLI Fellow at the Cleveland Museum of Art. Recently she was awarded the 2019 Toni Beauchamp Prize in Critical Art Writing by Gulf Coast Literary Magazine.

Sasha Kelley is a multidisciplinary artist, who's work centers the intimacy, incubation and social connection. As a co-founder and artist at The House of Malico, Sasha Kelley collaborates on projects/programs including Alignment Festival, Twerk 4 Mother Earth & Spectrum. Kelley's current practice includes event production, photography & performance. @on.mommas, analteredego, is used as a tool for subliminal medicine and emotional exploration—addition to a vibeyyy dj set. Sasha Kelley has exhibited at Siete Potencias Gallery, Krowswork, Somarts, and Berkeley Art Museum & Pacific Film Archive. Her works has been published in *Umber Magazine*, *Fader*, *Black Girl Magik*, *Staying Underground* & Lower Grand Radio

Michelle May-Curry is a Ph.D Candidate in American Culture at the University of Michigan, currently working as a visiting researcher at Harvard University. Her research focuses on photographic and literary representations of mixed-race Black-white families in the 20th and 21st centuries, charting how these representations change in relation to shifts in Black politics and aesthetics. Michelle has been recognized as a Bouchet Fellow, a Rackham Merit Fellow, a Humanities Without Walls Fellow, and received the Institute for Research on Women and Gender community of scholars research award. As well, she received a Bachelor of Arts in English and Political Science from Williams

College, where she was a recipient of the Creating Connections Consortium (C3) Mellon fellowship to conduct research at UC Berkeley. Most recently, as a Carr Center Independent Scholar Michelle collaborated with multimedia artist Carrie Mae Weems and other young artists and scholars to mount two art exhibitions in Detroit and in Cuba for the 2019 Havana Biennale.

Leigh Raiford is an associate professor of African American studies at the University of California, Berkeley, where she teaches and researches about race, justice, and visuality. Raiford is the author of *Imprisoned in a Luminous Glare: Photography and the African American Freedom Struggle* (University of North Carolina Press, 2011), and is coeditor with Heike Raphael-Hernandez of *Migrating the Black Body: Visual Culture and the African Diaspora* (University of Washington Press, 2017) and with Renee Romano of *The Civil Rights Movement in American Memory* (University of Georgia Press, 2006). Raiford's work has appeared in both academic journals and popular venues, including *American Quarterly*, *Aperture*, *Artforum*, *theatlantic.com*, *Ms. Magazine*, *Nka: Journal of Contemporary African Art*, and *Small Axe*. She has written catalogue essays about artists Dawoud Bey, Toyin Ojih Odutola, Lava Thomas, and Wendel White.

Renee Royale is an independent curator, artist, writer, and media strategist. She is the founder of *Support Black Art*, an online art platform that seeks to enhance the visibility of artists of the African diaspora. She enjoys increasing the accessibility and community awareness of experiences centered on contemporary artists of color.

Ricky Weaver is an image-based artist from Ypsilanti, Michigan. Though she is primarily associated with photographic works it is important that we understand her use of image in a broader sense (text, sound, thought, and reflection as image). Her practice postures a shared language between Black women in relationship to the quantum ontology of images as portals to elsewhere. She explores the idea of alternative modes of existence through themes of magical realism, the archive of the everyday, and dark sousveillance. She received her BFA in Photography from Eastern

Michigan University in 2014 and an MFA in photography from Cranbrook Academy of Art in 2018. Since then she has worked as Part-time faculty in the photography department at Wayne State University, Eastern Michigan University, and Washtenaw Community College. Weaver has participated in the Applebaum fellowship and Carr Center Independant Fellowship where she began her relationship with friend and mentor, Carrie Mae Weems. She has exhibited work in the 13th Annual Havana Biennial, The Photographic Center Northwest of Seattle Washington, The Beacon Project of Sacramento California, Page Bond Gallery of Richmond Virginia and more. Weaver has upcoming appointments as a visiting artist at the University of Texas, Austin in the Department of African and African Diaspora Studies and as a visiting artist in the photography department at Cranbrook Academy of Art.

Leila Weefur (She/They/He) is a trans-gender-noncomforming artist, writer, and curator based in Oakland, CA. Their interdisciplinary practice examines the performativity intrinsic to systems of belonging present in our lived experiences. The work brings together concepts of the sensorial memory, abject, hyper surveillance, and the erotic. Weefur has worked with local and national institutions including SFMOMA, The Wattis Institute, Berkeley Art Museum and Pacific Film Archive, and Smack Mellon in Brooklyn, New York. Weefur is a lecturer at the University of California, Berkeley and the San Francisco Art Institute.

Arisa White is a Cave Canem fellow, Sarah Lawrence College alumna, an MFA graduate from the University of Massachusetts, Amherst, and author of the poetry chapbooks *Disposition for Shininess*, *Post Pardon*, *Black Pearl*, *Perfect on Accident*, and *"Fish Walking" & Other Bedtime Stories for My Wife*, which won the inaugural Per Diem Poetry Prize. Published by Virtual Artists Collective, her debut full-length collection, *Hurrah's Nest*, was a finalist for the 2013 Wheatley Book Awards, 82nd California Book Awards, and nominated for a 44th NAACP Image Awards. Her second collection, *A Penny Saved*, inspired by the true-life story of Polly Mitchell, was published by Willow Books, an imprint of Aquarius Press in 2012. Her newest full-length collection, *You're the Most Beautiful Thing That Happened*, was published by Augury Books and nominated for the 29th Lambda Literary Awards. Most recently, Arisa co-authored, with Laura Atkins, *Biddy Mason Speaks Up*, a middle-grade biography in verse on the midwife and philanthropist Bridget "Biddy" Mason, which is the second book in the Fighting for Justice series. Forthcoming in 2020 from Foglifter Press, the anthology *Home is Where You Queer Your Heart*, co-edited with Miah Jeffra and Monique Mero; and in 2021, Arisa's poetic memoir *Who's Your Daddy?* will be published by Augury Books.

<u>Andrew Wilson</u> is a multimedia artist working in the intersections of ritual and funerary rights honoring the deceased, the ways objects accumulate spirit particles how these collide to open portals to different dimensions. His work is at once beautiful with an attention to craftsmanship and repulsing in its graphic subject matter. He wants to create an extra moment of counfoundment for the viewer to contemplate their relationship to the work and the imagery and histories it evokes. He received his BFA from Ohio Wesleyan University in 2013 with a concentration in Jewelry/Metals and his MFA from the University of California, Berkeley in 2017. Wilson's work has been in many galleries and institutions including: The Berkeley Art Museum, Yerba Buena Center for the Arts, SOMArts, and the Museum of the African Diaspora. He has received such awards and honors as: the Jack K. and Gertrude Murphy Award, an Emergency Grant from the Foundation of Contemporary Arts, the Carr Center Independent Scholars Fellowship, the McColl Center and more. He has also worked with Carrie Mae Weems on The Spirit that Resides in Havana, Cuba alongside the Havana Biennial and The Future is Now Parade for the opening of The REACH in Washington D.C. His work has been collected by Michigan State University and the University of New Mexico.

ACKNOWLEDGMENTS

Immense gratitude and love to Jamal, Leila, Ra Malika, nan, and Justin and Jacob from Wolfman Books for all of the commitment, energy and sweat.

Thanks to Sadie Barnette, Jamal Batts, Lukaza Branfman-Verissimo, David Brazil, Sarah Burke, Justin Carder, Anaiis Cisco, nan collymore, Ryanaustin Dennis, Estelle Ellison, Jade Ariana Fair, Courtney Fellion, Celina Garcia, Kathy Geritz, Ra Malika Imhotep, Christian Johnson, Darol Kae, Jacob Kahn, Sasha Kelley, Kevin Killian, Alima Lee, Spike Lee, Alli Logout, Tara Marsden, Summer Mason, Leonora Miano, Benjamin Michel, Ismail Muhammad, Shah Noor Hussein, Ed Ntiri, Chika Okoye, Yetunde Olagbaju, Numa Perrier, Brontez Purnell, Zoé Samudzi, Surabhi Saraf, Cauleen Smith, Soleil Summer, Shushan Tesfuzigta, Anisia Uzeyman, Leila Weefur, Jarrod Welling-Cann, Joshua "Bicaso" Whitaker, Andrew Wilson, David Wilson, Akande X, Neyat Yohannes.

And to BAMPFA, Betti Ono, Living Room Light Exchange, Nook Gallery, Qilombo, Real Time and Space, Southern Exposure, Spirithaus, The LAB, and Wolfman Books.

ABOUT THE BLACK AESTHETIC

The Black Aesthetic film series is about showcasing rare, independent, or unknown films and shorts that we think should have a wider audience. With each film viewing, we have a guided audience discussion where we tease out technical, structural, and socio-political themes in the films. The goal is to create a robust forum for people to exchange ideas, make connections, and experience the communal aspects of film.

theblkaesthetic.com